PENGUIN

CLAIRE ROBINSON

Illustrated by
Angela Hargreaves

Troll Associates

Library of Congress Cataloging-in-Publication Data

Robinson, Claire, (date)
   Penguin / by Claire Robinson ; illustrated by Angela Hargreaves.
      p.   cm. — (Life story)
   Summary: Describes different kinds of penguins and their physical
characteristics, habits, and range.
   ISBN 0-8167-2771-6 (lib. bdg.)   ISBN 0-8167-2772-4 (pbk.)
   1. Penguins—Juvenile literature.   [1. Penguins.]
I. Hargreaves, Angela, ill.   II. Title.   III. Series.
QL696.S473R63   1993
598.4'41—dc20   91-44727

Published by Troll Associates

© 1994 Eagle Books

Design by James Marks
Edited by Kate Woodhouse
Picture research by Jan Croot

Printed in U.S.A.

10 9 8 7 6 5 4 3

Picture credits
NHPA/ANT: 25
NHPA/N. A. Callow: 13
NHPA/Brian Hawks: 21
NHPA/Haroldo Palo: 19
Survival Anglia/Annie
   Price: 5, 7, 9, 11, 17, 27
Survival Anglia/Rick Price: 15
Survival Anglia/Mike Tracey: 23
ZEFA/E. Hummel: 29
ZEFA/Werner H. Muller: cover

INTRODUCTION

Penguins are popular animals. Their upright bodies and waddling walk make them appear almost human. But these black and white seabirds live far away, in lonely parts of the world where people seldom go. They cannot fly, but move with ease through the water as they dive for food.

This book will show you how they survive the cold, rough seas where they spend most of their lives. Then we will follow them ashore to find out where they lay their eggs and rear their chicks.

Penguins belong to the group of animals we call birds. One reason why penguins don't look much like birds is because they stand upright like people do. But the rockhopper penguin in the photograph has a lot in common with other birds. It has two feet and a tail, and a toothless horny beak for catching food. Like all birds, the penguin has a pair of wings, but it cannot use them for flying. Penguins lay eggs and rear their young. And, just like all other birds, penguins are covered in feathers.

4

Penguin feathers are short and dense. When a penguin grooms its feathers it spreads oil over them with its beak. This makes the feathers waterproof and keeps the penguin warm in icy seas.

After a year, the feathers wear out and have to be replaced. This king penguin is molting. It may take as long as thirty days for the shiny new feathers to push out all the old ones. While this is happening, the penguin feels cold. It cannot go into the sea to find food, because it is not waterproof. So the penguin stays on land and lives off the fat stored in its body.

The bright new feathers on the penguin's back are blue-black, and the front ones are as white as snow. Look closely at these three birds. Their bodies are similar, but their heads and shoulders are different. The tall ones with golden feathers are king penguins. The smaller bird is a chinstrap penguin.

There are 18 different species, or kinds, of penguins, and each kind has its own special head markings. These help the birds to recognize their own species and stay together. This is especially useful when they swim and only their heads show above the waves.

All penguins live south of the equator, but not at the South Pole, as you might think. Penguins are seabirds and the South Pole is over 800 miles (1,300 kilometers) from the sea, in the middle of Antarctica.

Emperor and Adélie penguins live in the coldest climates, on the shores of Antarctica. The Falkland Islands and South Georgia, in the Atlantic Ocean off the southern tip of South America, are home to millions of gentoo, rockhopper, and king penguins. The colony of king penguins in the photograph lives on South Georgia. But penguins also live on the southern coasts of Africa, Australia, and New Zealand, as well as the western coast of South America.

Penguins spend most of their lives in the water. The sea is where they find their food — fish and other sea animals. The water is cold, but penguins are kept warm by layers of fat and by their dense waterproof feathers.

Like all penguins, this king penguin is an excellent swimmer. Its smooth, streamlined body is perfect for diving. It uses its stiff, flipperlike wings to skim through the water, twisting and turning with its tail and feet. On long journeys, penguins swim underwater, but leap out every few seconds to take a breath.

On land, penguins are not so graceful. They waddle, using their wings to balance. "Tobogganing" is a faster way to travel. Some of the Adélie penguins in the photograph have flopped on their bellies and are pushing with their feet, sliding quickly over the snow and ice.

Climbing out of the sea is often difficult if there is no beach. Penguins swim close to the shore to take a good look. Then they dive down and shoot out of the water at great speed, landing on their feet.

After weeks at sea, penguins come ashore to rest, molt, and lay eggs.

When it is time to breed, adult penguins journey home to the rookeries where they were born. Usually the males arrive first, often returning to the same nesting place as the year before. Soon there are thousands or even millions of penguins in the rookery, each choosing his own private space to nest in.

This gentoo has scraped a shallow bowl in the ground with his feet. Now he is collecting pebbles and building up the sides of his nest. If his neighbors come too close, there will be an argument. Sometimes when he is not looking, they might steal his stones.

A few days later, the female penguins arrive. The males become very excited and call loudly to attract their attention. Now the rookery is really crowded, and the noise is deafening.

This male chinstrap penguin is performing a courtship display to find a mate. He lifts his wings and stretches his neck toward the sky, calling loudly. Soon a female waddles up and greets him. She is probably the same female who mated with him last year. She hasn't seen him for months, but amazingly she can recognize his call above all the noise.

The two birds continue building the nest together.

Several days after mating, the female penguin lays her eggs — usually two. The eggs must be kept warm for at least five weeks while the chicks grow inside. The male gentoo in the photograph is nudging the eggs gently with his beak toward a bald patch of skin near his feet. Here the eggs will be kept warm by his body.

While the father penguin cares for the eggs and lives on the fat stored in his body, the mother goes back to sea to eat. When she returns, many days later, she greets her partner with a bow and the two birds change places. Now the hungry father can eat, too.

One day the penguins hear a small cheeping sound inside one of the eggs. It is time for the chick to hatch. It uses a special egg tooth on the end of its beak to make cracks in the shell. Then it pushes the shell apart with its feet. The broken pieces are blown away in the wind. Right away, the tired chick nestles down close to its parent. Soon afterward the second chick hatches. They are both covered in soft, fluffy feathers that protect them from cold wind and blizzards. Most chicks are pale gray, while king penguin chicks are brown.

For three weeks the chicks stay in the nest close to one parent, while the other parent collects food for them. The chicks grow quickly and, as their appetites get bigger, both parents have to go to sea to fetch enough food. While the parents are gone, all the chicks in the rookery gather together in a large group called a crèche, like the gray emperor chicks in the photograph. They huddle together for warmth and to keep safe from their enemies. If a chick wanders away from the crèche, it may die of cold or be attacked by a skua, a large seabird.

The penguin parents come back from the sea with food. But how do they manage to find their own chicks in such a crowd? They call out to them! Both parents and chicks recognize each other by their voices.

Stretching upward, the chick pecks at its mother's beak to beg for food. The female brings half-digested food up into her throat. The chick then puts its head right inside its mother's beak to eat.

Soon the chicks lose their coats of fluffy down and grow adult feathers. Now they are mature enough to plunge into the sea for the first time and find food.

Once in the water, the young penguins must learn to catch food for themselves. Darting and diving, they follow schools of fish and squid that rise to the surface at night. The cold Antarctic seas are full of small, shrimplike krill, a favorite food of penguins.

The sea is a good place to find food but it can be dangerous. Giant petrels swoop overhead, looking for weak or young penguins, while hungry leopard seals lurk in the waters below. Despite the dangers, the young penguins leave their parents and head for the open sea.

Fascinating facts

The world's largest penguin is the emperor penguin. It is 45 inches (115 centimeters) tall. The smallest is the little blue, or fairy penguin. It is 14 inches (35 centimeters) tall and lives on the coasts of New Zealand and southern Australia.

30

emperor penguin

Adélie penguin

fairy penguin

Penguins cope well with the cold. Their problem is overheating! In strong sunshine, they fluff their feathers or stand with their wings outstretched to cool down. Most penguins living in warm climates, such as the Humboldt penguin living off the coast of Peru, nest in burrows to keep out of the sun.

The Galapagos penguin lives on the sun-baked islands where the sea is cool, just south of the equator.

Emperor and king penguins do not build nests. They incubate their eggs on their feet under a flap of skin.

Penguins have about 70 feathers per square inch (10 per square centimeter).

Penguins are rather short-sighted, but see better underwater. They have excellent hearing.

Index